In Search of Lady Jane

Richard Clements

The Larks Press

Published by the Larks Press

Ordnance Farmhouse, Guist Bottom, Dereham NR20 5PF

01328 829207

May 1998

Printed by the Lanceni Press, Fakenham

British Cataloguing-in-Publication Data

A catalogue record for this book is available from the British Library.

ISBN 0 948400 69 2

Acknowledgements

This account of the loss of an aircrew over Norwich and the story of the short time they spent at Horsham St Faith could not have been compiled without the help of many people:

The staff of the Second Air Division Memorial Library, Norwich. Their help and enthusiasm has not waned over the years despite the disastrous fire which resulted in the total loss of the Memorial Room.

The family and friends of the air crew, particularly Mr and Mrs Gilbert Dooley, Mike and Cindy Quirk, Bill Gorman, Hilda Jarvis, John Gagnon and Ruth Pegg.

Tony North and Mike Bailey, here in Norwich, who so willingly and patiently introduced me to the B 24 Liberator and its many different models. Also for allowing access to what is probably the world's most comprehensive collection of Second Air Division photographs.

George Reynolds, the historian of the 458th Bomb Group in the States, for his tireless enthusiasm despite my constant flow of questions over the years.

The former members of the 458th Bomb Group, Rick Rokicki, Gerry Allen, Alex Shanoski and Thomas Wholley Jr.

John Thompson, 401st Bomb Group.

John Trueluck, 56th Fighter Group.

George Plunket for access to his vast photographic collection.

Christine Armes for her work in tracing the crew's families.

The many people of Norwich for their willingness to share their war time memories.

Finally John Kowalczuk Jr. and Burton Wheeler Jr. Had it not been for them, the story of 42-95133's final flight could not have been told. Someone once said to me during a transatlantic phone call, 'You sure meet some great people along the way'. I have had the pleasure of getting to know two such people.

Richard Clements, Norwich.

Plate 1. The Tuns Inn, Unthank Road
The buildings on the left stood on Chapelfield Road

Introduction

During November 1944 an aircraft accident occurred in Norwich, which in itself was not unique, for there were a dozen or so aircraft crashes in or around the city during the war. Some, for example the crash of a B24 *Lassie Come Home* at the Boundary, had more tragic consequences for the people of Norwich. What makes this one different is that the crew's desperate struggle was witnessed by so many. A large number of people saw the crew battle for control of the aircraft over approximately one mile, at roof-top height. For many it was the most memorable incident of the war.

The aircraft, a B24 Liberator J4-95133 K was returning to Horsham St Faith from a practice mission when it struck the 95ft. tower of St Phillip's Church in Heigham Road. It then flew on for approximately 1,000 yds. to crash in the corporation yard off Barker Street, just under 2 miles from the end of Horsham's runway 35.

Friday 24th November 1944 was cold and drizzling, typical of many November days. Ruth Taylor had left off work earlier that afternoon to keep a dentist appointment and was now, at just before five o'clock, walking home. Being double British summer time it was still daylight as she walked up St Giles, crossing over the road at the Tuns Inn. Standing on the corner she looked up and saw a large American aircraft, a Liberator. She recalls, 'It was flying very low, in a sideways manner, over Earlham Road. The plane was obviously in serious trouble, it was making a horrific noise and appeared to have smoke coming from one of the engines. It lost height and disappeared from view. Within a few moments came the awful sound of the crash. This was followed by numerous explosions and the sound of what appeared to be gun-fire. I realised then that if the crew were still on board they would have no chance of surviving.'

Ruth continued her journey home; the weekend was just beginning and she was due to keep her regular date with a young American navigator. Some weeks before, they had been introduced by the padre of the 458th Bomb Group. She remembers, 'He loved being with my

Plate 2. Ralph Dooley with his crew at Topeka, Kansas, August 1944.
Standing Left to Right: S/Sgts. Oscar B. Nelson (waist gunner), Paul A. Wadsworth (radio),
Don P. Quirk (waist gunner), Ralph von Bergen (tail turret), John J. Jones (engineer/gunner),
John A. Phillips (nose turret).
Kneeling Left to Right: 2/Lts. Burton Wheeler (co-pilot), Ralph J. Dooley (pilot),
John Kowalczuk (bombardier), Paul E. Gorman (navigator)

Photo via Hilda Jarvis

family and soon grew very fond of my father; they used to laugh together a great deal. He liked being part of a family and involved himself with family activities. On one occasion he helped my father clear out the garden shed.' As time went by he and Ruth spent more and more time together, attending some of the tea dances held at St Andrew's Hall. Occasional evenings would be spent having a drink in the Bell Hotel. It was on one such evening he introduced her to his pilot, Ralph Dooley. 'He, (Ralph) struck me as very mature for his age. I felt that under the happy and carefree exterior there was a serious young man who could handle most situations with calmness and competence.'

Ruth did not realise as she stood on the corner at St Giles' Gate, watching the stricken aircraft, that Paul Gorman, the young navigator to whom she had become very, very close was a member of the crew. Her life was about to take a completely different direction.

Ruth's worst fears for the safety of the crew were realised, all nine had perished in the disaster: the pilot Ralph Dooley, stand-in co-pilot Arthur Akin, Paul Gorman the navigator, John Jones the engineer and top turret operator, Paul Wadsworth the radio operator, waist gunners Oscar Nelson and Don Quirk, nose gunner John Philips and the tail gunner Ralph Von Bergen.

This was, however, not the crew that had trained and flown together until the day of the accident. Two changes had been made. First, the crew were without their bombardier John Kowalczuk, for he had been transferred off the crew during the week before the crash. Secondly, Arthur Akin had replaced Lt. Burt Wheeler as co-pilot. Akin was a first pilot in his own right and a close friend of Dooley's. They had known each other during their training and had been assigned to Horsham St Faith with their respective crews at the same time.

Training and Trucking

The crews had been formed during early May 1944 at Biggs Air Force base, El Paso, Texas. Key personnel arrived on orders from previous assignments, trained pilots, bombardiers, engineers and gunners. On 5th May the crew was listed as: Dooley, Wheeler, Kowalczuk, Jones, Wadsworth, Von Bergen, Nelson, Bistis and Fili.

It was on the train from Lincoln, Nabraska to El Paso that Burt Wheeler first met his pilot, Ralph Dooley. Ralph had been called to active duty on February 13th 1943 and commissioned Second Lieutenant February 8th 1944. Burt Wheeler was called at the end of January 1943 and also commissioned Second Lieutenant in February 1944.

John Kowalczuk takes up the story. 'Our B24 training began at Biggs Air Force Base. I was aware that Dooley and Akin knew each other before they showed up at Biggs. I must say a few words of Dooley the young freckled face kid of 19. He was very pleasant with the crew in conversation and passed out compliments at the right moment, an intelligent young man who knew how to handle an emergency. He enjoyed smiling with the fellows and those around him. By the way I was the only married person and at the age of 26 the oldest on the crew.'

'As bombardier my first flight with Dooley was on May 13th, I had a total of 47 lasting some 122hrs, of this figure 21½ were at night. My final training flight was on July 17th. Dooley would have had to have flown some additional hours with a skeleton crew that included co-pilot, engineer, navigator and radio operator to familiarise themselves with the aircraft. During one flight one of the guys had a bad case of diarrhoea. Having used the available paper bag the bomb bay doors were opened and a drop occurred somewhere over the barelands of Texas.'

By 26th July two gunners, Matthew Bistis and Dominick Fili had been replaced by Quirk and Phillips.

At the conclusion of their training, August 3rd, the crews were transferred to Topeka, Kansas. Dooley's crew was assigned Shipment FC-900-BA 80 and Akin's FC-900-BA 78 to fly

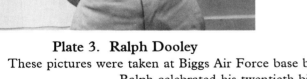

Plate 3. Ralph Dooley   Plate 4. Burt Wheeler

These pictures were taken at Biggs Air Force base by John Kowalczuk in July 1944 not long after
Ralph celebrated his twentieth birthday on the 9th of June.

new B24s over to England. However some crew members were late for the essential formation
and other crews took over. As a result the crews were shipped to Camp Kilmer, New Jersey and
from there to New York to board the troop ship U.S.S. Alexander. Crossing the North Atlantic
took approximately one week. After landing at Liverpool they were first shipped to a replace-

meant depot at Stone from there over the Irish Sea to a camp on the outskirts of Belfast. On August 26th 1944 the crews were assigned to the 753rd Squadron, 458th Bomb Group, 96th Bomb Wing, 2nd Air Division of the 8th Air Force. Back across the Irish Sea they came, and by train to Norwich.

After arriving at Horsham, numerous flights were made, both before taking up combat missions and during stand-down periods from them. Burt Wheeler recalls these 'could be group practice, individual crew practice, slow timing a new engine after an engine change, ferrying a general around, night or instrument flying time. We did all of these.' John Kowalczuk recollections on these flights, as bombardier, included 'work on bombing runs on established targets with explosive white powder bombs.'

During the second half of September the 458th had their operational missions suspended. The aircraft were stripped down to essential equipment, with bomb bay and wing drop tanks installed within the aircraft, thus enabling a total of up to 1,662 gallons of gasoline to be carried. All three bomb groups of the 96th Wing took part in these 'trucking' missions. Their purpose was to transport fuel required for Patton's forces in France. Three main airfields were used Lille, Clastres and St Dizier. Akin, probably with a reduced crew, took part in a total of five, four to Lille and one on Saturday the 23rd September to St Dizier.

Meanwhile Dooley, with a limited crew consisting of Quirk, Wheeler, Wadsworth, Gorman, Von Bergen and Jones, had a flight to Lille on the 23rd returning the next day, 24th. On the 25th they did the round trip to Lille and back in one day.

On the 26th John Kowalzcuk went along for what turned out to be an eventful ride. During the flight over to Lille, Paul Gorman decided to check out his dead reckoning navigation. Burt Wheeler remembers 'I was flying at 3,000 feet and as we made landfall I saw tracer shells from the ground passing just a few yards in front of the plane. Following them down, I saw a quad 20mm anti-aircraft gun in the street below busily trying to shoot us down.'

'We now knew we had failed to make landfall over the intended friendly territory but were not sure why. We made the course-change normal for a flight to Lille and held a hasty

Photo via Alex Shanoski

Plate 5. Arthur Akin with his crew at Topeka, Kansas, August 1944
Standing Left to Right: T/Sgt. Alex E. Shanoski. 2/Lts. Charles W. Hall (bombardier), William B,
Cheney (co-pilot), Arthur C. Akin (pilot), Dale G. Dunham (navigator).
Kneeling Left to Right: S/Sgts. Herbert D. Ballou (tail turret), Paul P. Fellner (waist gunner),
Richard C. Eggleston (ball turret), Chester E. Calis (radio), Walter Kray (waist/nose turret)

Plate 6. U.S.S.Alexander

flight deck conference. As an additional complication to the fast on-coming dark we realised we did not have the colours of the day which might allow a safe return to the base in England. We knew the British antiaircraft crews were nigh perfect with all the practice on V1s. Return was a very risky option.'

'We had circled during this time and saw a C-47 Dakota cargo plane heading south east and decided to follow. It was lost in the dark almost immediately. Then we saw a single strip of lights below indicating a possible runway. I flashed our landing lights and received a green Aldis lamp signal in return. Dooley then proceeded to make a fantastic safe landing in the dark on this strange field.'

'The lights turned out to be globular kerosene lamps such as were used to mark highway construction, a single row of them. How Dooley decided which side of the row to land on I cannot remember. The field was sod, with no paved runway, a British Typhoon base. They welcomed us and said they expected to be bombed later that night. They offered a map and a course to Lille but it was refused. Enough was enough for one day and we caught a ride into Brussels.'

John recalls, 'The surface of the runway was rough with bomb craters on both sides and only 3,000 ft. long, but we were down safely and damn glad to find out where we were. We created a lot of excitement with the British who saw the first B24 loaded with gasoline land on such a treacherous strip. *[This airfield is believed to have been B-56 Evere, occupied at the time by 127 Wing 83 Group. Other airfields in the area were B-60 Grimbergen and B-58 Melsbroek occupied respectively by 131 Wing 84 Group and 139 Wing 2nd Group.]* The aircraft was not capable of taking off because of the load, so arrangements were made to unload the petrol. They had to find the necessary equipment to handle it and the best thing they found was a manual pump. It would be a long process to empty those tanks so in the mean time they made a real effort to transport us to down-town Brussels. After what we went through it was a blessing to be around for a celebration.'

In Brussels complications continued. Earlier there had been a troop-landing by glider and the pilots had been very slow about making their way back to areas where they could be transported back to England. As a result the town Mayor had orders not to assist flight personal with food or quarters and there were no exceptions.

John recalls 'We stayed one night, September 26th, at the Metropole Hotel and paid the bill with cigarettes. Cigarettes also set two of us up with draft beer at Wielemans Lounge nearby. Had a grand time with the crowd.'

The men returned to the airfield the following afternoon to find the fuel was still being unloaded; it was then that Burt Wheeler suggested the possible use of the plane's fuel-transfer pump located in the bomb bay. This speeded things up, however they were still not ready to take off until the following morning, the 28th.

A considerable audience turned out to watch takeoff, sitting on the wings of the

Plate 7. Trucking Mission

Lille, France, 24th September 1944, showing the crew
on the second day of their first trucking mission.
Left to Right: Oscar Nelson, Burton Wheeler,
Paul Wadsworth, Paul Gorman, Don Quirk,
John Jones, Ralph Dooley.

Typhoons waiting to see if they would be successful. Burt Wheeler explains that 'we had to use all the short field takeoff techniques we knew, lifting one wing over the tail of a B-17 Fortress which had crashed some time earlier and then the other wing over the chimney of a burnt out house. Back at base no concern had been felt. They thought we probably suffered a mechanical problem at Lille. The cause of this? John had not been briefed for a strong up-channel wind. We had intended to make landfall at Ostende which was in allied hands. Instead we were blown up to Zeebrugge which was still German controlled.'

On Monday October 2nd the group had been stood down. Akin and his crew were taking part in a practice mission, flying the group assembly ship *Spotted Ape*. For the mission Akin and his co-pilot, Al Cheney, had swapped places. On takeoff the number one engine caught fire, burning a hole in the retracted wheel. After one circuit of the field they landed, however the tyre burst immediately on impact. In the resulting crash Dean Ballou, the tail gunner, was injured though not seriously.

Combat Missions

The two crew's first combat mission was on Saturday, October 7th. Two of a total of 29 aircraft from Horsham put up that day, the target being Magdenburg's Rothensee oil refinery. All did not go well for the new crews. Burt Wheeler remembers that Dooley, flying J4 134 R, had to use near takeoff power whilst climbing to altitude over the North Sea. Realising the fuel would not last to complete the mission he aborted.

Arthur Akin and his crew, flying J4 449 WO, were also experiencing problems. Lt. Dale Bunham, the navigator, and permanent sufferer of air-sickness, ran out of oxygen. As a result Akin broke formation and went down to 12,000 ft. He landed at a Fleet Air Arm field on the coast to take on more gas before returning to Horsham. Aircraft J4 133 K did take part in this mission and was flown by Lt. Fuson and his crew.

Also taking part in their first combat mission that day was George Wheeler, Burt's older brother. Flying with the 331st BS 94th BG their target was the oil installations at Bohlen. George and his crew were one of 26 to take off from Bury St Edmunds that morning, however only 14 were to reach and bomb the target.

Plate 8. Arthur Akin

Photos via Alex Shanoski

Plate 9. Al Cheney

An account taken from *Lingering Contrails Of The Big Square A*, a history of the 94th Bomb Group, describes events leading up to the bomb run:

'*All went well until about 12 minutes before the initial point. Suddenly from the high cloud cover emerged 50 or 60 enemy fighters with obvious destruction on their minds. Single and twin engine planes were scattered in apparent disarray as they came in from the rear. In waves of eight to ten aircraft, they pressed home their attacks. After firing at very close range they split up, peeling left and right with a few ducking under the formation and executing a split S.*

It all happened in seconds, but in spite of the shock, guns were firing and the radios crackling in every B-17. As suddenly as it began it was over. Gunners claimed two fighters destroyed, four damaged and one probable. The fighter escort responded immediately, but time was insufficient for an effective counter-attack. While still stunned, formation leaders requested damage assessment. George Wheeler and his crew in 'The Sprit of Valley Forge', 42-102616, flying number five position in the low squadron were observed on fire and going down.'

Photo via Cliff Hall

Plate 10. The Spirit of Valley Forge
The B17 George Wheeler flew on the Bohlen mission of October 7th. One of eight aircraft lost by the 94th Bomb Group that day

Dooley's next mission was on the following Monday, the 9th. The target for the group's 29 Liberators was the marshalling yards at Koblenz. On this mission, lasting 5 hours 35 minutes, the group encountered some light flak. It was reported by some crews during de- briefing that vertical contrails were seen over the island of Schouwen from 22,000 ft. at 13.43. seemingly inclined towards England.

Thursday October the 12th, Akin took part in the Osnabruck mission. His crew was one of twenty from Horsham. Eleven of the crews could not locate the target and did not release their bomb load.

On Friday 13th the group was scheduled to take part in a mission to Cologne, however due to bad weather the mission was scrubbed. Some of the crews from Horsham took this opportunity to have practice missions during the afternoon. Burt Wheeler's log shows that he had a 4 hour flight that day.

Saturday 14th both Dooley and Akin with their respective crews were to be part of a force of 33 put up by the 458th to bomb the previous day's target of marshalling yards at Cologne. Dooley in aircraft J4 133 K and Akin in J4 134 R. The aircraft were parked on hard stands 40 and 47 respectively. The two young men would have been facing each other, separated only by the perimeter track as they went through their pre-flight checks.

The flak on this mission was more accurate and Dooley's aircraft suffered some minor damage, one Liberator from St Faith's was hit and seen to drop out with one engine smoking. Akin was forced to abort when Paul Fellner, one of his gunners, developed severe stomach pains.

Andy Anderson, a radio operator with another one of the squadron's crews, kept a diary of his missions from June 14th through to December 27th. Some of these coincided with Akin and Dooley's, the Cologne mission being one. His entry for the day read in part, 'Clouds over target, flak intense but we were lucky until we got to the franklines. Then all hell broke loose, Simpson got it through the left leg, so cold the blood froze as fast as it came out -33° C'.

Sunday October 15th, all three Air Divisions of the Eighth were bombing oil production targets in the Monheim area. Akin and his crew were twelfth out of eighteen to take off from Horsham's runway 23 in aircraft J4 066 Y. It was reported that during the mission six of the group's aircraft were 'crowed out' by the 266th. Bomb Group so did not bomb. The remaining twelve had good results.

13

Thursday October 19th. Both Dooley and Akin took part in the mission to Mainz. The twenty crews put up by the 458th bombed the secondary target, marshalling yards. John Kowalczuk's record of missions shows that they dropped their 250lb. bombs from 25,600 ft. The mission lasted 6 hrs 30 min. Some flak was reported but the group suffered no losses.

Akin's sixth mission was on the 22nd October when he took part in the mission to Hamm. This time the aircraft he flew was J4 980 V. J4 133 K did take part in the mission, on this occasion piloted by Richard Alvestad.

Dooley had to wait a full week for his next mission, when on Thursday 26th the crew took part in a raid on the Mittelland Canal. They formed part of a force of 242 B24s, 29 from Horsdham. The target was an aqueduct which carries the canal over the river Weser. Releasing their 2,000lb bombs from 19,200ft. through thick cloud the results went unobserved. The effects revealed by later reconnaissance were reported in *Target Victory*:

'MINDEN CANAL JACKPOT'

'Minden's chokepoint on the Mittelland canal-most important waterway between the tank and armament factories of Central Germany and the Western front-was smashed to a dead stop by the 2AD Libs on Thursday. The entire mission was PFF, above 10/10th clouds, from base to target.

A 2000lb direct hit tore an 85-foot breach in the canal wall at a key point where the waterway stands 20ft above the terrain. Water rushing from the canal swept four huge barges and a tug boat into adjacent fields-one at least 400 yards from the canal. Two and a half miles of the canal were drained, and at least 15 barges and tugboats are stranded without a drop to float on.

Thru this area at least 300 vessels normally operate daily, on the most important east west waterway inside Germany. The Mittelland canal connects Berlin with the Ruhr Valley and the Rhineland.

Due to allied bombing of oil plants and rail centres, curtailing highway and railroad transport, this waterway is vitally important to the Germans. Its connecting link thru the Ruhr, the Dortmund-Ems canal, was breached by the RAF on September 23.'

Monday October the 30th Akin and his crew were one of thirty from Horsham to take part in a major mission, again oil production targets. All three Air Divisions of the Eighth were taking part. However due to deteriorating weather the First and Third divisions were recalled to seek secondary targets. The participating Second Division groups managed to reach their primary, which for the 458th was the oil refinery at Hamburg.

Andy Anderson notes on the day's mission read, 'Take off was at 0930, target Harburg, six miles south of Hamburg. Around 150 (anti-aircraft) guns in the area, we were in range of them for 6 min. temp -40° C, landed 15.30.' The group suffered the loss of one aircraft on this mission.

Thursday 2nd November Dooley was again in aircraft J4 133 K and one of 30 liberators to take off from runway 05. The day's target was the railroad intersection at Bielefield, however, due to a mechanical failure on the lead aircraft, the group released prematurely, bombing a canal.

Plate 11. Spotted Ape
The group's second assembly ship seen here leading a formation which includes 'SOL' and
'.........KAY SPECIAL'

Saturday 4th November Akin took part in the Misburg mission, the day's target being oil installations. Breaks in the cloud revealed that results were poor with all hits about six miles east of target.

Andy Anderson noted in his diary that there was 'more talk about having to do 35 (missions), hope it is just a rumour.' When America first entered the war their crews had to do a 25 mission tour, this was increased to 30 and, as feared by Anderson, eventually 35.

Monday 6th November Akin and his crew were one of twenty-eight from Horsham to return to the Mittelland Canal. The target was again the aqueduct. Observations indicated that great efforts were being made to repair the damage caused by the November 26th mission. However, all the shipping was still at a stand-still.

Andy Anderson's notes on the day revealed 'Take off at 0750, landing 1330. Minden, Germany. Aqueduct over river, a canal that was pretty important. Flak intense, at Musfors when we drifted off course. Left wing man got it pretty bad. We got it in the left wing and nose.'

On the 9th November, a day that would end in confusion and disaster, the group dispatched 25 aircraft to the Metz area in support of the U.S. 5th Division. The mission was to assist them in their drive by bombing emplacements and German positions along the front line about 6 miles S.S.E. of Metz. This was to be an all out effort by the Eighth; all three divisions were hitting targets in the same or adjacent areas. Only 12 of the 25 458th aircraft attacked the assigned target.

On this occasion Dooley was flying J4 163 M, *Time's A Wastin*. The crews were awakened by 0300 with takeoffs starting before 0700. Dooley would have taxied out on to the perimeter turning right passing Wood Farm to position himself in line at the end of runway 23. After take off he was to assemble and take up position in the low left squadron. Whilst approaching the target area the bombardier of one element of their squadron had an early release of the bomb load with other aircraft making releases at the same time. Consequently a large explosive pattern occurred on their own troops, inflicting heavy casualties.

As a result of this serious mistake many of the crews were denied a credit for the mission. Also the group's Distinguished Unit Citation awarded in September 1944 was revoked. However, on the day, General George S Patton praised the actions of the Eighth Air Force. He notes in *War As I Knew It,* 'Visiting the front on the ninth was very disheartening. Many bridges were out; trucks, airplanes, and one hospital platoon were marooned by the flood waters, and things looked bad. However, when I got to the 5th Division, General Irwin, Division Commander, and Colonel A.W. Roffe, Commander of the 2d Infantry, and myself went up on a hill and saw 1476 planes of the Eighth Air Force come over and bomb the targets at Metz. It was great sight. At first we saw smoke corkscrews in the air, and some of us thought they were German anti-aircraft rockets. Actually they were markers from our lead planes. We were close enough so that the roar of the motors was very distinct, and the ground where we were shook constantly.

Generals Spaatz, Doolittle, and Curtis, and Professor Bruce Hopper, historian for the Air Force, spent the night. I was grateful to them, because I am quite sure that the wonderful air support we had received that day was due largely to the friendship of these men.'

Gerry Allen was scheduled to be tenth to take off, flying J3 602 A in the same Low Left Squadron. However he recalls; 'The original aircraft I was assigned was not in condition to fly and we had to switch to one of the mission spares. Being very late to take off, I was only able to catch the end of the bomber stream and wound up with a composite group of stragglers which included both B 17s and B 24s. Hence I wasn't with the 458th over the target. I did receive a credit for this mission.'

Andy Anderson on Lt. Vincent's crew also took part in this mission and in the same squadron. They were scheduled to take off fourteenth, four behind Dooley. Anderson noted in his diary that it 'was as cold as the devil' when the crews were roused. As a result of the confusion his pilot made a run on the target on his own. However their problems were not over as a bomb became hung up and was later dropped in the Channel. He concludes his account of the day by saying 'Flew back by ourselves, it was snowing when we landed.' He noted that this was his 27th mission.

John Kowalczuk was a member of the 10th Infantry, 5th Division before transferring to the Air Corps. This was to be the last mission he was to have with the crew. He takes up the story. 'I was taken off the crew by the 753rd Squadron Bombardier at my own request. I wanted to perform as a real bombardier and not as a 'Toggle Switch Operator'. I did that on four or five missions with Dooley who did not want to take up the lead position. He wanted to go home as soon as possible by flying off the wing tips. Get 35 in and you're on the way. I made a strong remark to the head man. Whom I met for the first time that day, by stating either have me fly as a lead bombardier, or send me back to the Infantry to do a man's job.'

This was a common frustration with bombardiers for having trained on the Norden bomb sight they then seemed relegated to a switch operator, watching for when the lead aircraft dropped his bombs to do the same. Earlier in the war each aircraft was responsible for establishing its own bomb run, aiming and release. It was found that if this was left to highly qualified crews, flying as squadron and group lead, a tighter bomb pattern could be achieved.

On November 16th, after a lay-off for a number of days due to bad weather, Akin and his crew were one of 33 from Horsham assigned another supporting role for the ground troops. The day's target was a rough area of land approximately 1,400 yards square, located two miles N.N.W. of the centre of Eschweiler, ten miles north east of Aachen. The area contained gun emplacements and troop concentrations. At time of takeoff it was dubious whether or not the mission would get off the ground. The weather report at 1030 read 'sky obscured, visibility 500yds. fog'. However due to the importance of the mission the go-ahead was given. When the crews arrived back over the UK they were diverted due to fog. Akin, on what turned out to be his last combat mission, landed at Blyton.

Dooley's final combat mission was to Hamburg on 21st November. He was assigned aircraft J4 285, *Table Stuff*, and was 25th out of a total of 28 to take off from runway 05. The day's target was the oil refinery at Rhenania-Ossag.

Plate 12. Table Stuff

The aircraft Ralph Dooley and his crew flew on their final combat mission to Hamburg on November 21st. This is also the aircraft used on a number of occasions by Akin's crew with their replacement pilot Lt. Robert Eidelsberg

19

24th November

Following the Hamburg mission, the group was stood down for three days due to poor weather over the continent. On the 23rd Burt Wheeler received news that his brother, George, was missing in action. He explains, 'My first word was a V-mail letter from my dad. At that time the only contact with my brother had been by mail using APO numbers. After receiving the V-mail letter the 458th tower told me where his group was located.'

The two brothers had been called to active duty at the end of January 1943. Both had taken the exam for aviation cadet the previous autumn. They did their basic training at Atlantic City, New Jersey, then on to College Training Detachments Classification to be trained as pilots, Pre-flight, Basic and Advanced Twin Engine Training. Burt explains 'We were both to be in Class 44-B (February 1944) to receive our commissions and wings. George needed an operation while at Advanced which delayed him into 44-C. I visited him at his base before returning home on leave. This was to be the last time we were to meet.' George Wheeler went on to become a B-17 pilot with the 94th Bomb Group flying from Bury St Edmunds, having first married his school sweetheart six week before going overseas.

'The next morning, the 24th, checking with Squadron Operations I was informed a practice mission had been scheduled and had not been scrubbed. My reply as I remember was "even the birds are walking". I could not believe they would run a practice mission in that weather.' (*The purpose of the practice mission was for pilots to gain more experience on instrument flying. Ralph Dooley had, over the previous six months logged 10 hrs. 20 mins.. Over the previous 30 days, 4 hrs. 45 mins.*)

'Most of the flying officers up to the rank of captain were quartered in the Combat Officers Mess building. As relatively new arrivals, we were overflow and quartered in housing on the other side of a large field and across a lane that ran through the base towards Catton. Each crew had two rooms with two officers to a room. My recollection is that Akin's crew was next to Dooley's, I woke Arthur Akin up and asked if he would fill in if they did fly the practice

Photo via Tony North

Plate 13. Horsham St Faith's Station 123 in 1947
The aircraft at the top of the picture is Spotted Ape. In the distance is Rackheath airfield. Runway 35
is nearer the bottom of the picture running from right to left roughly parallel to the Holt road

mission. He readily agreed and I went off to my brother's base.'

In the late afternoon of Friday 24th the weather at Horsham was recorded as 'ceiling 500 foot, visibility 2 miles, temp. 47, wind N.W. 13 knots, pressure 29.24 with intermittent drizzle'. Alex Shanoski, Akin's Flight Engineer, explains that for them it was an off duty day, a day spent in the barracks playing cards, catching up with the letter-writing and laundry.

Alex was in the barracks when the mission came in. 'It was a real mess. The planes had all their lights on and were just overhead missing the roof tops. They couldn't find the end of the runway. We could hear the planes and briefly see them as they disappeared into the low clouds. There was then a brilliant flash of light on the Norwich side and we knew one of our planes had crashed. We rushed over to the operations office were we learnt it was Dooley's crew with Arthur Akin on board. He didn't have to fly that day, he just loved to fly.'

One report, taken from the group's history, said:

'As the aircraft returned to the base the weather had closed in and it was a question whether our boys would get down safely. The field personnel were certainly sweating them down that day. Overhead the aircraft were flying at almost building level and in a somewhat broken pattern. It was eerie to look up, see a black shape, and landing lights so near to the ground. One felt as if he could almost stand on the roof of one of the buildings and touch the planes as they went by. Without letup, flares were being fired in an effort to help the boys locate the runways. One by one they landed and soon there were but a few still flying in the muck. Lt. Dooley attempted a landing but overshot the field. He took off, trying desperately to gain altitude but could not".

George Reynolds, the 458th group historian and author of The 458 Bombardment Group History, explains the situation Dooley would have found himself in.

'When Dooley made his first landing approach it would have been to runway 35, the shortest but the one equipped for instrument landings. He would have slowed the aircraft down to just above flying speed. Then when he decided to abort the landing, and go round, he would have to apply a lot of power as well as deepen the pitch of the props. Also the

22

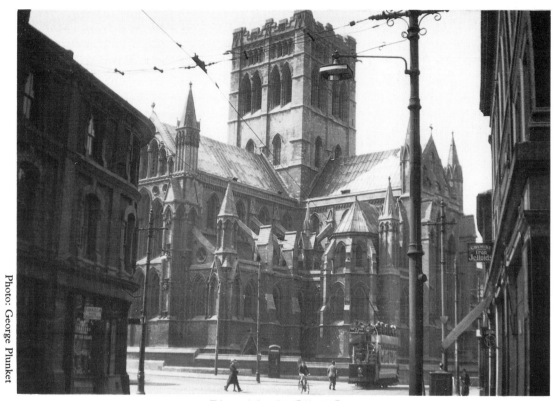

Photo: George Plunket

Plate 14. St Giles' Gate

The junction of Upper St Giles, Earlham Road and Grapes Hill. It was in this area of the City that the aircraft was first noticed in distress. The photograph shows St John's Church with St Giles' Gate Stores public house on the left. The Tuns Inn is just around the corner to the left and the bank where Peter Bence would often sit is round to the right. This early photograph by George Plumket was taken on the 3rd of February 1931 when trams still ran up Earlham Road.

policy was any time an aircraft flew, all its fuel tanks were full on takeoff. Thus even though they had flown for some unknown time there was still a lot of weight in fuel.

Under these circumstances, many pilots will attempt to keep the field in sight and remain beneath the clouds to shorten the landing procedure, especially in deteriorating weather. That is rather than climb back into the clouds and set up the full instrument landing sequence, they remain clear of the clouds and make a visual approach. Forward visibility in an aircraft is much less than one's standing on the ground. The base observer reported 2¼ miles visibility, but I doubt that Dooley had any more than a mile at most aloft and of course he was also watching about a dozen instruments. The aircraft altimeter being one that could have been in error on true altitude and they were actually lower than the instruments indicated. However no one will know for sure. I doubt if he ever saw the church.'

Recent research carried out in Norwich suggests that Dooley had a problem which was unobserved by base personnel. The accounts were given by a number of people in the St Giles Gate area, who saw the aircraft before it hit the church tower.

One was Les Huckle, sixteen at the time, on his way home after calling at Williments model shop in St Benedict's. He takes up the story, 'I was walking up Grapes Hill and had almost reached the top at St. Giles Gates. With a full view of St John's Catholic Church in front of me, I heard the almost deafening roar of aeroplane engines. I looked up and the huge shape of a Liberator appeared over the top of St John's Church tower. The plane was so low it almost touched the tower and seemed as big as the church itself. I could see that one of the starboard wing engines had stopped as the propeller was stationary. It passed over my head and went down towards Dereham Road. The plane was in a nose-up angle as it came over the church and remained at that angle till it passed from my view, but it was losing height all the time.'

John Southgate was on his cycle and had stopped at the traffic lights at the top of Grapes Hill. He describes the aircraft in what appeared to be a steep dive as it broke cloud over St John's church. 'I could clearly see the port inner engine was smoking and on fire,' he says.

Both John and Les must have passed each other that day - unknown to them then that a few years later they were to join the City Police together and, after several years, retire at the same time. However, during their careers they never mentioned the aircraft to each other.

P.C. John Fletcher had just come off duty and was walking home down Earlham Road As he reached the junction with Heigham Grove he heard the roar of engines above and describes what he saw. 'A large U.S. aircraft appeared from the direction of Earlham Court flats flying very low. It crossed Earlham Road and disappeared over the tree tops at the junction of West Pottergate and Heigham Road, then reappearing, gaining altitude and banking over the area of City Station goods yard. It then banked sharply and went into a steep dive and disappeared from view.'

Shirley Crocker, then aged 12, was living in Heigham Grove and remembers it vividly. 'My mother and I were standing talking in our hall, and were suddenly brought to a halt by the loudest noise overhead that we had ever experienced. So much so that we both put our hands over our ears and cowered in fright. We were quite convinced that the plane was going to take our roof off, it was so close.'

Mrs Ward was walking home after attending the clinic on Earlham Rd., when she became aware of the aircraft circling; as she passed St Phillip's church it struck the tower. She recalls 'Pieces fell all around me but I didn't get hit, there was only one other woman there and she went hysterical.'

Reverend Eric Griffiths was in St Phillip's vicarage at the time; he did not see the aircraft, but did hear it. 'As I got to the door a part of the wing was bounding up the drive; a few seconds after came the explosion. Part of the tail came to rest on the other, north, side of the nave.'

Ray Fisher was standing outside Southgate's grocery store that was on the corner of Golding Street and Dereham Road. He first saw the aircraft immediately after it struck the church. 'It was facing up the Dereham Road towards Bowthorpe Road, explains Ray, in a very high (between 30 and 40 degrees) nose-up attitude with approximately 12ft. of the right wing and most of the aileron missing. The engines were on full power but the aircraft was flying sideways across Dereham Road towards Heigham Street. After climbing sideways the aircraft stalled, the right wing dropped and the plane rolled on to its back. The total time between hitting the tower and the crash was no more than 20 seconds.

That afternoon the young Peter Bence was on a frequent perch of his in the roof of a bombed-out bank that stood at the top of Earlham Road, next door to the Grapes Hotel. From here with the aid of a pair of broken German binoculars he would sit and watch the coming and going of aircraft from Horsham.

He recalls, 'I saw a B24 flying towards me and noticed it was unusually low, slightly to my left and trailing smoke. A few seconds later I could see fire around a port engine. I could clearly see a crew member leaning out of the port side waist window, he appeared to be looking at the fire or getting air. The aircraft then began to veer away from me to my left, almost over-head. I could see there were bits falling off, some on fire. It then went out of sight but I could still hear it and the sound of minor explosions.

To my surprise it came back a few minutes later, this time it was very low indeed flying in the opposite direction and much closer, I seemed to be looking down on to it, by now very much on fire. I next remember seeing a huge fireball and hearing a very loud explosion. I jumped down into the loft, scrambled out of the building and ran down Grapes Hill into Barn Road. At the Heigham Street junction I saw people running towards Old Palace Road. I could see lots of smoke and hear the sound of ammunition exploding. As I ran along Heigham Street a fire engine passed me. I reached the site of the crash and squeezed through the crowd. As I did so I heard a police officer or air raid warden shouting to us to keep back. The last sight I had of the aircraft was an engine with the undercarriage sticking out.'

Michael Flood was one of a group of young lads playing in the trees that stood on the junction of Earlham Road and Recreation Road. 'I remember the aircraft came from the city flying above the Earlham Road. We all looked up. Being only nine years old it seemed to be flying just above the houses; one thing I can remember is seeing one of the crew looking out

Plate 15. Heigham Street junction with Old Palace Road

A Norwich Street scene which has changed beyond all recognition, not a single building shown here remains standing today. First left is the entrance to Home Street, second left Paddock Street, third left Barker Street. This is one of a number of photographs taken by Burt Wheeler's parents during a visit to the U.K. between the 10th and 14th July 1954.

27

of the side window. It passed over us, then I lost sight of it as it went behind the houses. A little while later we heard the bang. We all thought it had come down in the cemetery but later heard it crashed in Heigham Street, so we all went to have a look. It was as we walked down Heigham Road that we noticed the wing up against the church tower; to me, being small, it seemed like the whole wing stood there. When we got to the crash it was just a mass of flames, I was looking through the large gates when the fire engines came from the base.'

Gladys Wodehouse, a member of the Royal Observer Corps, was in her house at 22 Derby Street when she heard the Liberator low over the city. 'You could tell it was in trouble because of the noise it was making. I was with my neighbour at the time so we both ran out into our back yard. It was then we heard the crash as it hit the church. We stood and watched it fly almost on its side towards City Station. We felt so helpless just watching as the crew struggled with the aircraft.'

Hazel Dade was playing in her garden at number 55 Clifton Street with some younger friends when she heard the noise of the approaching aircraft. 'I looked up and there it was just above roof-top height. We all threw ourselves to the ground as it went over us. As I looked up I noticed it had a piece of the tail hanging on about 10 ft. of wire that hit our chimney and broke the pot. I could clearly see the crew, one of which was at the side window looking out. It then swerved around the factory and in doing so appeared to turn over. After the crash we all ran over the building site that was to be Causeway close, but were stopped going into Barker Street by the vicar, Reverend Lanchester.'

One of the first on the scene was Ken Yaxley who first saw the aircraft when he was cycling down Heigham Road. 'I had just turned in from Earlham Road when the aircraft came over the Black Horse pub, it was very low. I saw it hit the church, it seemed only a glancing blow. I then raced along Heigham Road and down Old Palace Road. As I turned into Barker Street I saw a U.S. service man arguing with the yard's gate keeper, who was not going to let him in the corporation yard. Well the American hit him and ran in to see if there was any thing he could do. The aircraft was a mass of flames and from what I can remember was about 25yds. inside the yard and over to the left.'

Plate 16. Barker Street
A picture clearly showing the gates remembered by so many of the witnesses. Burt's mother,
Bella, is seen talking to Mr E. Edwards outside 31 Barker Street.
The gate-keeper's house, No. 37, is just inside the yard.

Olive Hutson was in West End Street. 'I was thirteen at the time but can remember it as if it was yesterday. I used to love doing my mother's shopping and always used to go to Dashwood's shop in West End Street. As I came out of the shop I looked up to see the plane; it was making a horrible noise and was very low.

I remember one of the wings were broken and it was on fire. I called to Mr Dashwood and he came running out. You could see it was going to crash and then it went down. I had two sets of grandparents, aunts and uncles living down Barker Street so I ran down there. The police were stopping people going in to the street, so I explained to them my grandparents lived down there so they let me go. It was a terrible sight, just a ball of fire. Lots of men who lived down there ran into the yard to see if they could help in any way, but they couldn't get near. It's a miracle how it missed the houses; it went down just inside the yard.'

Vera Read was working at Harmer's factory in Heigham Street. The building was only recently, 1996, demolished. 'I was on the third floor facing the window when the aircraft plunged by, I feel sure it was in flames. How the pilot missed the tall building I don't know. I remember hearing the muffled crash above the machinery noise. It all happened so quickly I don't think many workers actually saw the plane as they all had their eye on the machine needle.'

Doug Mallet remembers his aunt telling him that she was at work in the Pearl Laundry looking out a rear window when she saw the plane fly along the backs of the houses on Old Palace Road. As it approached the laundry it turned over just scraping over the roof.

Earnest Pratt, was just leaving his butchers shop on the corner of Railway Street when the aircraft plunged by in flames. He remembers the heat from the fire overhead was frightening. After the crash he was one of several men who tried to help from the Barker's Street side. However, the heat was so intense and with the numerous explosions they just could not get close enough.

Michael Yallop had just walked out of the sweet shop on the corner of Sayer Street and Heigham Street when the aircraft appeared overhead. At that moment a man, who was cycling past, jumped off his bike and threw him up against a wall for protection, fracturing his arm in the process.

Brian Coleman and a colleague, Peter Yardy were working at Soman Wherry Press, in Heigham Street. Brian says that towards the end of the afternoon the whole workshop was lit by a red glow and rocked by an explosion, which brought Tom Barry, his manager, running through. Tom, who had a son in the R.A.F., asked them to get outside and do whatever they could to help. The two young men ran out the back of the printing works, along the side of a dyke and into the City Station yard. From there they had to run up the tracks and through the coal yard; at that time he remembers coal was piled alongside most of the tracks. Upon arriving at the site they saw that two or three of the crew were outside the aircraft, lying in the centre of a large spillage of burning fuel. In a desperate bid to answer their screams for help they crawled to within 40-50ft. of the aircraft, but because of the intense heat and the many explosions they were unable to reach any of the airmen. Frustrated by their inability to do anything they had to pull back.

It was about this time that they noticed the arrival of the National Fire Service (N.F.S.) who approached from Barker Street through the large gates to the yard. Access for the fire appliances appeared hampered by the fire, numerous railings and the large piles of coal. The fire crews were unable to get around to the same side as the men. Bill Batson, a member of the N.F.S. crew at the time, recalls the sight as the most horrific he witnessed during the war and remembers the three men. Sadly they had perished by the time they had brought the fire under control enough to reach them. Also attending was Mr Wortley, a member of the City's Civil Defence and Rescue Service. He responded with a rescue party from a depot at the Eagle baths in Helford Street arriving on site at 1706; his report in part read 'Was called to crashed aircraft, arrived at incident and found aircraft a mass of fire, stood by for 20 min. As there were no houses or civilian casualties and no hope of reaching the crew I returned to depot.' The time was 1735.

The sound of the crash and sight of the pall of smoke attracted a group of young lads,

Plate 17. Norwich Corporation Depot

The crash site being surveyed by two airmen, probably on the 25th. The piles of coal over which Brian Coleman tried in vain to reach the crew can be clearly seen to the right of the track.

who were playing in an alleyway between Wingfield Road and Bakers Road. One of them was Brian Clayton who says 'I was 11 at the time and playing in a group with about 9 or 10 friends. When we heard the crash we ran out into Wingfield Road and down on to St Martin's where we had a good view overlooking the site. After some time a group of four U.S. ambulances and fire trucks turned into St Martin's from Aylsham Road. They crossed over Drayton Road and, seeing the fire down to their right, started to turn into what is now St Martin's Close, not realising they were on the wrong side of the river. It was as the first truck turned that a boy I was with ran across and jumped on to a truck's running board. Grabbing the wing mirror arm he redirected them round by Oak Sreet, City Station bridge and down Heigham Street. By the time we had run round they had closed off Barker Street.'

Burt Wheeler remembers; 'On return from my brother's base the Dooley crew rooms were dark and empty. I started across the field toward the combat officers' mess and happened to meet John Kowalczuk who told me Dooley's plane had gone down and the flight surgeon wished to see me.'

Tributes to the way Dooley handled the aircraft were soon being made by the people who witnessed the incident. The following day the Eastern Daily Press carried the story on the front page. It reported that eye witnesses said that the manoeuvres of the plane gave the impression that the pilot was making every effort to avoid crashing on a heavily built up area. Over the next few days several letters were published in the press. One from Mrs E. Notley was typical.

'Sir, I and others would like to pay tribute to the pilot and crew of the American bomber who did their very best to avoid crashing among us and to express our deep sympathy to the relatives of the men who were lost. All the people who saw the plane admired the way the pilot handled the situation and thereby saved many lives.

The crewmen's funeral took place on Wednesday November 28th at 3 p.m. with full military honours at the Cambridge cemetery.

Residents of the Heigham Street area provided a plaque in memory of the crew. It was

Plate 18. St Philip's Church drive
Another in the series of photographs taken by
Burt Wheeler's parents. Part of the tower
dislodged by Dooley's aircraft can be seen
on the left.

unveiled by the Lord Mayor, Mr E.F. Williamson, in the presence of Brigadier General E.C. Kiel on Tuesday November 6th 1945. In his speech the Lord Mayor said that this was in no sense a city function. It belonged entirely to the people of the district. It was the result of a spontaneous thought of gratitude and admiration arising in the hearts of the people who lived there. At the moment of their own great peril the men they remembered thought of others.

In 1972, due to redevelopment, the plaque was moved from its original position on the wall of 196 Heigham Street, the then home of Mr Jermy, to its present site on the wall of flats on the junction of Old Palace Road and Heigham Street, the site of the old Pearl Laundry.

St Philip's church, built during the 1870s, was demolished in November 1977 regardless of the fact that it was a grade II listed building, and despite moves by the Norwich Preservation Trust to save it. On November 2nd 1977 the church commissioners reported that after a three year wrangle over the building's future they were ready to accept a tender for pulling it down. The Preservation Trust claimed to have produced a viable alternative to demolition which involved turning the building into eleven homes. 'To

Plate 19 The Unveiling of the Memorial Plaque

The Lord Mayor of Norwich, Mr E. F. Williamson, unveiling the memorial plaque on 6th November 1945. Standing behind the Lord Mayor is Brig. General E.C.Kiel, who served as Deputy Commander of the Eighth Air Force under Lieut. General J.R.Doolittle. The photograph shows the plaque in its original position on the wall of 196 Heigham Street.

demolish the building when there is a feasible alternative must rank as vandalism in excelsis', they declared.

John Kowalczuk went on to become a lead bombardier and completed 18 missions, his last on April 18th 1945. After the war he became a reservist 1st Lieutenant and was recalled into ervice in February 1951 until October 1953, ssigned to 7th Air Division in England as an

Plate 20. Bella Wheeler at the Plaque in its original position
At the time this photograph was taken, July 1954, Sydney Arnup ran the corner shop and occupied
No. 196 Heigham Street.

Air police Officer, promoted to Captain and then back to reserve status. After 9 years of active duty and 17 years reserve in the Infantry, Anti-Aircraft Artillery and the Air Force he retired. Lt. Col. Burt Wheeler was assigned co-pilot with James Kelly and his crew. By VE Day he had completed a total of 28 combat missions. After being released from active duty in 1945 he returned to work for the Mann Company. Upon the death of David Mann in 1957 the company was acquired by the GCA Corporation and Burt Wheeler became General Manager of the David Mann Division and a Corporate Vice President. He retired in 1983 after 43 years service.

Akin's crew was assigned a replacement pilot, Lt. Robert Eidelsberg. Their final mission was to Wilhelmshaven on March 30th 1945 which ended a tour of 35 missions. Alex Shanoski explains that for most of their missions they flew the B24 named *Table Stuff*. 'It was a fine aeroplane except number three engine would periodically catch fire, frightening everyone on board and on other aircraft. It had an oil leak whereby the oil would collect inside the cowling and fall on the red hot supercharger, flames would flare out past the tail and beyond. It would only last a few seconds so we no longer feathered and shut down the engine.'

On March 14th 1945 the aircraft which they were scheduled to take on a mission was involved in an accident whilst still on the ground. 'Our planes were fully loaded with 500 incendiary cluster bombs,' explains Alex, 'and parked on their hard stands around the perimeter track in preparation for a mission. An over-zealous gunner in an adjacent aircraft loaded his gun with a belt of 50 calibre ammunition, the gun inadvertently went into automatic fire. The bullets ricocheted off the tarmac and into our aircraft. No one was hurt fortunately, but it was the most beautifully exploding B24 you ever did see.'

Just how much control Dooley and Akin had over the aircraft we will never know and it would be both unwise and unfair to speculate. However, even after more than 50 years, there are still people who, like Mrs Notley, maintain that their actions saved the lives of many. Olive Ashford, then Olive Hutson, writes, 'The crew gave their lives, but they saved lots of others. Their families can be really proud of them all.'

Plate 21. Freeman Square
Some of the the 300 people who attended the memorial service conducted by the Revd Michael Jones
on November 24th 1994.

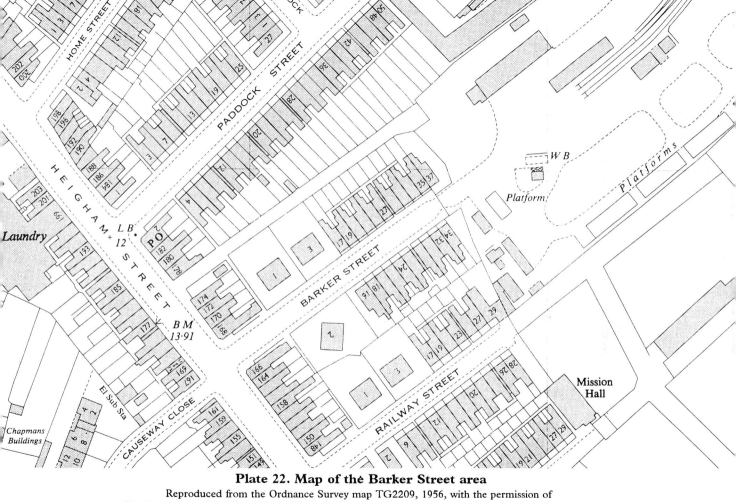

Plate 22. Map of the Barker Street area

Reproduced from the Ordnance Survey map TG2209, 1956, with the permission of
The Controller of Her Majesty's Stationery Office, © Crown Copyright Licence No. MC88230M0001.

39

The Crew

2/Lt. **Ralph J Dooley**, Pilot, aged 20. Ralph graduated from the Northeat Catholic High School, Philadelphia, PA. in June 1942. For a short period, about nine months, he worked for the Penna Railroad. He was drafted into the army on February 13th 1943. On February 8th 1944 he was commissioned 2/Lt.

2/Lt. **Arthur C Akin, Jr.** Pilot, Portsmouth, Virginia. Age 22.

2/Lt. **Paul E Gorman**, Navigator, aged 23. Paul graduated from James Madison High School, Brooklyn, New York 1938. He was employed as a newspaper advertising manager in Sussex county before enlisting in the army on October 1st, 1942. On November 14th 1942 he received the non-commissioned officer's rank of corporal. During January 1943 whilst with the Signal Corps at Fort Monmouth New Jersey, Paul made application for appointment as aviation cadet. He trained at Nashville, Tenn., and San Antonio. In July 1944 he was commissioned Second Lieutenant.

S/Sgt. **John J Jones**, Engineer/Top Turret, Gem, Texas. After leaving school John was a farm and ranch worker. Upon entering service he became an aircraft mechanic at Gulport, Missisipi. He saw service in Florida, Michigan, New Jersey, Pearl Harbour, Utah, Nevada, California and Texas.

S/Sgt. **Paul A Wadsworth** Radio Operator, Forsan, Texas

S/Sgt. **Oscar B Nelson**, 24, Waist Gunner, from Vashon Island, Washington. In 1940 Oscar enlisted in the Coast Artillery and after leave in 1943 he enlisted in the Air Corps.

S/Sgt. **Ralph Von Bergen**, 21, Tail Gunner, Denver, Colorado. Ralph graduated from the West High School and joined the air force in January 1943.

S/Sgt. **John A Phillips**, 23, Nose Turret. John graduated from Norwood High School, Norwood, New York in 1941. He entered service on October 10th 1942 and received his basic training at camp Robinson, Arkinsas. On December 10th 1942 he was sent to the Aleutian Islands where he was stationed until October 10th 1943. Returning to the states John was sent to Laredo, Texas to gunnery school.

S/Sgt. **Don P Quirk, Gunner**. Don graduated from Central High School Muncie, Indiana in 1938. He worked for the American Railway Express before entering service in October 1942. Don spent two years in the Panama Canal Zone returning to the states for leave in November and December 1943. Assigned to the air force, he trained at Biloxi, Missisippi, Panama City, Florida, and Lincoln Nabrasca, where he received his wings in May 1944.

After the war and at the families' request most of the crew were returned to the States for private family burials. Today only Donald Quirk and Ralph Von Burgen remain buried at the Cambridge Military Cemetery.

Photo via Mike Bailey

Plate 23. March 14th 1945 -'The most beautifully exploding B24 you ever did see.'

J4 42-95133 K Lady Jane ?

The name *Lady Jane* has, for a number of years, been attributed to the aircraft Dooley flew on the practice mission that day. However no conclusive evidence has emerged in support of the name. J4 95133 K is mentioned in a number of books and on lists as having this name. As to where the connection of 95133 to Lady Jane originates nobody can recall. John Kowalczuk is sure the aircraft they used on a regular basis did not have a name.

Photographic evidence is inconclusive, for as yet no clear photograph of the aircraft has come to light. One photograph shows a number of B24s from Horsham in flight. In the middle distance is a Liberator of the right type, from the 753rd squadron and with what appears to be a 'K' call sign on the tail. No nose art is visible.

The record card for 42-95133 reveals that the aircraft was made by Ford at Willow Run and delivered to the USAAF on 17th March 1944. It was assigned to the Eighth Air Force, arriving in England on 30th April. The aircraft travelled via Nashville, Birmingham Alabama (where it underwent some modifications), Topeka and Bangor Maine. It was usual for aircraft upon arriving in the UK to undergo further modifications before assignment to a bomb group. 95133 was the probable replacement for another 753rd BS aircraft *Kiss Me Baby* which also carried the J4 K markings. This aircraft, 44-40264 crash landed in England on 5th September 1944.

By this stage of the war no bomber crew was permanently assigned one aircraft; as has been seen 95133 had a number of different crews. Over the period of time that Dooley was at Horsham the 458th flew a total of 29 combat missions. A name could be associated with any one of the other crews or the crew who ferried the aircraft over from the States. Upon arrival in the UK, aircraft and crew usually went their separate ways.

A number of theories have been put forward as to the source of the name. The *Daily Mirror* was at the time running a cartoon strip which featured a scantily dressed Jane. It has also been suggested that the name originated from *Lady Chatterley's Lover*, first published and available in the States during 1928.

Plate 24. J4 42-95133 K, Lady Jane?
To date what is thought to be the only photograph of the aircraft Ralph Dooley and his
crew flew on November 24th

And of course, many aircraft were named after loved ones back home.

Bits and Pieces of the Mighty Eighth lists four other heavy bombers with the name Lady Jane:-

Serial Number	Bomb Group	Bomb Squadron
251188		36
Unknown B17G	447	
338607	401	613 H
2107009	401	613 H

Second Lieutenant John Thompson was the co-pilot on Lt. Vermeer's crew with the 401st flying from Deenethorpe. John explains 'on 18th March 1945 we were assigned the B17 G *Lady Jane II* for a mission to Berlin. All did not go well, we were shot down by a ME 262 on our way back. Lt. Vermeer and three other crew members were killed and the rest of us ended the war in Stalag Luft I at Barth, Germany.'

Other Lady Janes within the Eighth include the P-47 of John 'Lucky' Trueluck, a 63rd FS ace with seven kills to his credit. As a member of the 56th FG he flew from Horsham St Faith's during May and June 1943. After moving to Halesworth early in July he was assigned a new P-47 and named it *Lady Jane* after a young lady from Texas who would later become his wife.